THE COURAGE OF A SINGLE FRECKLE

JUSTIN K. DODSON, PhD

WINDFALL PUBLISHING

Copyright © 2020 by Justin K. Dodson, PhD All

rights reserved.

No part of this book may be reproduced in any form or by any electronic or mechanical means, including information storage and retrieval systems, without written permission from the author, except for the use of brief quotations in a book review.

ISBN-13: 978-1-7348568-1-1 (Paperback edition)

ISBN-13: 978-1-7348568-0-4 (Ebook edition)

CONTENTS

DEDICATION

CHAPTER ONE
THE COURAGE OF A SINGLE FRECKLE……………………………….1

CHAPTER TWO
EDUCATION DIDN'T MATTER…………………………………………….3

CHAPTER THREE
ARE YOU LISTENING?……………………………………………………..6

CHAPTER FOUR
CAN I LIVE?………………………………………………………………….8

CHAPTER FIVE
MY SKIN YOUR FEAR…………………………………………………….10

CHAPTER SIX
INDIA ARIE SAID IT BEST……………………………………………….12

CHAPTER SEVEN
DELAYED AWARENESS………………………………………………….15

CHAPTER EIGHT
"MR. JUSTIN, YOU BE FRESH"…………………………………………17

CHAPTER NINE
I CAN'T WIN FOR LOSING……………………………………………….19

CHAPTER TEN
THE DANGER OF A SINGLE STORY-MY FACE…………………….20

CHAPTER ELEVEN
SEPTEMBER 19, 2016……………………………………………………24

CHAPTER TWELVE
SOCIAL MEDIA AND A UNIFORM………………………………………26

CHAPTER THIRTEEN
RAISING A SON……………………………………………………………28

CHAPTER FOURTEEN
ANGER..31

CHAPTER FIFTEEN
CONVERSATIONS WITH A YOUNG BLACK MAN......................35

CHAPTER SIXTEEN
WHAT DO I DO WITH THIS MESS?..37

CHAPTER SEVENTEEN
I LITERALLY HATED HIM: VALUES & HATE...............................39

CHAPTER EIGHTEEN
CONTINUING THE CONVERSATION: SOLUTIONS......................43

This book is dedicated to you, the reader. If you are reading this book, may you always do the following:

1. Love who you are.
2. Allow yourself to be human.
3. Don't apologize for things you did not contribute to.
4. Find every opportunity to laugh.
5. Accept the things you cannot change.
6. Express gratitude daily.
7. Keep putting one foot in front of the other.

1

THE COURAGE OF A SINGLE FRECKLE

I have always defined courage as remaining who you are even when the world around you wants you to be something else. I even have a tattoo on my right rib to show it. It says, "I am courage, I am truth, and I am me." It is a reminder to myself and others that I have my own truth, and with courage, I can be myself. My mother hates seeing me with tattoos, but I believe my tattoos have meaning and were carefully thought about. After all, if you are going to endure that type of pain, it better be important to you.

Accepting myself has been such a difficult struggle for me. From growing up wanting to be white and disliking my skin complexion, to thinking being white was automatically associated with being rich or simply made you better than others. I no longer believe those things; however, I do think there is an automatic abundance of privilege for white people that lead to more resources and opportunities compared to people of color. I won't harp on that subject in this book, but this does present an opportunity for others to identify where they see their own privilege.

On the next page, identify when and how you first recognized you had privilege, and what does it entail? Some examples of this could be able-bodied, owning a car, having an education, food security, feeling safe, having resources, or being proud of the culture you come from.

As a child growing up, I remember asking my mother if white people smelled, and she responded by saying, as only she could, "Baby, white folks can get funky just like Blacks can." For some reason, I had a distorted belief that white people were superior to Blacks in every way. Depending on what lens you look through and how you define superior, the ideas I had as a kid might be somewhat true. As I've grown, I've seen the advantages white people are afforded. But as a kid, I gave the idea too much credit. Now that I think of it, maybe superior was the wrong word to label my thought; perhaps, more widely accepted, liked, or respected could capture more of the truth. White people are definitely not superior, and as an adult, I know that no one is superior to anyone else. We are all the human race (whether Trump thinks so or not). Do you agree or disagree with this statement?

2

EDUCATION DIDN'T MATTER

Returning to Memphis to live full time after undergraduate and graduate school in 2013 was a game-changer for sure. At that time, I was about 24 years old. It was then that I experienced my first racial profiling. A friend of mine and I went walking in Midtown Memphis. Like most people just coming out of graduate and undergraduate programs, I didn't have a lot of money, and I had depleted my funds moving back to Memphis for a job. I was too embarrassed to admit it, but I could only afford a walk-in Midtown if I wanted to catch up with him. On this particular day, I wore a Henley shirt, black and white Chuck Taylors, a beanie, and glasses. Pretty non-threatening, right? Not everyone agreed with me because, as we walked, we began to see the police drive around. At first, I didn't think much of it. I remember thinking, "Wow, this is a really good neighborhood watch." Little did I know I was being watched as I walked with my friend in the neighborhood.

Eventually, the police approached us in a car. The officer drove up to us and asked, "Have you guys seen anything suspicious around here?" We naively answered in unison, "No, sir, we haven't." But as we continued walking, I couldn't help but notice the cop car following us. I saw the officer talking with someone and I realized it must have been the man who called the police on us. I couldn't help but think he looked far more suspicious than us.

I had just graduated from Lipscomb University as the first African American male with a master's degree in Professional Counseling. I had made history, made my mom proud, and blazed a trail. But coming home and being racially profiled taught me no matter how many degrees I have, what school I attended, or how nice my mom is, some people will only see my skin color. It was also a lesson for me to start genuinely experiencing my skin color for what it was. I needed to understand what my skin color meant to others but mostly to myself.

Is it weird that I felt compelled to judge him back? Is it because I felt judged; my natural response was to do it in return? Was this the Memphis in me coming out? To feel safe and protected, you talk about the other person to make yourself feel better or to save face.

However, there is no "saving face" when you're up against a monster like racism. Think about how we talk about monsters. Children have their parents look under the bed or in the closet to make sure the monster isn't there. Why? Because it will "get them" if it is. Children want the monster gone, to be safe, to be assured, to be able to sleep. That is how I look at the monster of racism. I want it gone so I can feel safe, assured that if something terrible happens, it isn't due to hate.

It's interesting because I remember thinking the man who reported us looked suspicious due to him being unkempt and dirty looking, not because he was white. However, my friend and I were well-groomed and judged based on skin color. I'll let you think about that one. I remember driving home angry, first because I was hot (it was a Memphis summer after all). Secondly, because I was appalled, the police thought I was a threat to society.

Now that I am a bit older, I can't help but wonder if it would have made a difference if they knew anything about me other than my skin color. The truth is, people judge others before they are allowed to reveal the good in them. Must people show something good as a get out of jail free card to not be judged? I don't think this should be the norm, but I know it's not fair that we—yes, I said we—all judge other people. Even more unfair, it justifies our actions of judging people based on their appearance—instances like calling the police on my friend and me when we didn't exhibit any threatening behavior. I guess the only threat presented were two Black men spending time in a place he believed we did not belong.

Have you ever been racially profiled or experienced being mistreated? If so, how did you respond? What did you do with that emotion? If not, how have you remained safe?

_____
_____
_____
_____
_____
_____
_____
_____
_____
_____
_____
_____
_____
_____
_____
_____
_____
_____
_____
_____
_____
_____
_____

3
ARE YOU LISTENING?

When I was in graduate school, I realized discussions of race made people who aren't Black uncomfortable. It was in my career counseling course when Dr. Hamley asked the class, "What do you tell a client who comes to you and says, 'I did not get this position because of my race?" One classmate instantly talked about a time where he had to cover his tattoos for a job; a second classmate stated that she had to cut her hair due to private school. I said, (which drew the attention of the entire class), none of that has to do with race. A different classmate retorted that it is his job to challenge a distortion. I challenged back with a question: How much could you challenge what YOU think is a distortion before you become disrespectful? Because at that point, you're challenging someone's reality. Especially if perception is reality, right? The classmates evaded the original question. I reminded the class that I couldn't change my skin color any more than someone can change their DNA.

    Contrary to popular belief, being Black can have its perks. People are going to pay attention to you. Whether they are scared of you, have low expectations of your ability, or simply being nosey, you have their attention. Now it's up to you to decide what you will do with this attention. Either we choose at that moment to live down to their expectations as African Americans and prove them wrong or decide not to care. But a decision must be made. It was at that moment I knew I had their attention, and it was my responsibility to help them understand the original question. "What do you tell a client who says they did not get the job because of their race." My classmates, who had minimal experience with minorities, needed to know that sometimes they would come across people who have experienced discrimination. They would discriminate against others if they failed to listen, were too quick to respond before truly understanding the situation, or if they failed to acknowledge their own preconceived beliefs. My classmates evaded a question they either did not know how to answer or never considered having to explain. What do you do when you have the attention of others? Are you mindful of how you present yourself? What do you think others think of you when you walk in a room before you say anything?

4
CAN I LIVE?

Now, if I had a hidden camera in my car watching me daily, someone would think I was a psychopath, or I didn't have friends. I am not the only person who sings loud, has full conversations, and yells at other drivers. Either way, the one constant is that I enjoy playing my music loudly. Loud enough that I'm sure I disturb others around me. There have been times in life that I would pull up to a red light, and if someone white were next to me, I would turn my radio down. My thought process was that I didn't want to disturb them because they would judge me. The reality is, there was a probability that I was going to be judged no matter what.

I've gotten away from trying to cater to others. However, I do believe being Black comes with responsibility. My mother always taught me *to be careful about how you carry yourself because someone is always watching.* I'll continue to balance that concept with not caring about what everyone thinks. At some level, I think we should care what people think (employers, parents, mentors, your children, etc.) but the general public? Not so much.

Do you care what others think of you? How do you balance honoring your values and not being consumed with the opinions of others?

_____
_____
_____
_____

5
MY SKIN, YOUR FEAR

As a child, I remember my father would tell my brother and I stories about white women clutching their purses or holding their children closer to them when they saw him. I remember he said at some point in his life; he had a job that required him to go door to door. My father said that people would slam the door in his face or not open the door due to fear because he was a large Black man. I believe it is the responsibility of people of color to consider what factors besides our race; we may internalize as rejection. Nonetheless, I am sure he was rejected due to his size and skin color.

Little did I know that one day I would experience similar experiences. I have walked past cars and can hear the car doors lock, and I've felt the need to stay away from young white children in public because I don't want any trouble. It can be quite comical at times and offensive at others because I know I am in no way looking to harm others.

Where does that fear come from? Is it media, society, or generational culture? Is the fear unmerited? In graduate school, my classmate Mike said he experiences the same rejection because he is a larger, bearded male. I'm not a large man, so I couldn't help but feel frustrated at his response. In moments like this, we often find ourselves wanting someone white or someone we think doesn't accurately share our experience, to feel less justified by their complaint. The reality is, he has somehow felt rejected by others. It is not my place to take that away from him because I believe my experience was worse. I can simply allow my experience to be mine and his experience to be his. The two don't have to compare.

When have you felt rejected by size, race, different ability (disability), or religious belief? What did you do with the emotion?

6
INDIA ARIE SAID IT BEST

At the age of 27, I decided to let go of what I thought I had: my hair. Yes, I know, so serious, right? Well, the middle of my head was bald, and my hairline was tugging at the back of my neck. My friend Shaneá would often encourage me to shave my head, but I denied the need to for quite some time. I would even get my haircut really short to try and blend it, so it wasn't as noticeable. Who was I kidding? It was time to accept the inevitable. Besides, Rogaine itched, and I could not afford to buy those fancy infomercial pills. So, I shaved my head, and it was one of the most liberating experiences ever. It boosted my confidence, and I received great responses from my loved ones.

At this same time, I began my doctoral program at an urban university in the southeastern part of the United States. A few days after shaving my head, I decided to shave it myself because a professional did the initial cut. I listened to the advice of men who walked the green mile and had head shaving down to a science. I trusted them. Their instruction was about to save my life, or so I thought. WRONG!

I did exactly what they told me to do: I got the same razor, shaving cream, followed the steps and it backfired BAD. The back of my head resembled concrete for a week. This caused me to wear a hat backward to class. Wearing it like this covered most of my head, and I preferred the look.

I met with my professor before class wearing my hat, and he didn't utter a word about it. Once class began moments later, he looked at me with the attention of my class and asked, "Why do you look like a homie?" My Black class member initially said, after lowering her head, "You can't say that." He proceeded to use other words such as "bro" to describe how he thought I looked with a backward hat. Meanwhile, I was simply trying to cover an allergic reaction in the back of my head. Some women came to class with their hair disheveled, but nothing was said about them. It only leaves me to think that he said this to label me.

I challenged a white male in my class to wear his hat backward one day to see the type of response he would elicit from the same professor. My classmate instantly assumed the professor would say something but denounce him for wearing a hat with a logo of an NFL team, the Bears on it. Of course, that didn't make me feel any better, as that comment would be a jab directed at the team rather than what my white friend resembled while wearing his hat on backward.

When I was younger, I wanted to be white or light-skinned because I believed that society (which at that age consisted of other kids) appeared to view people with lighter complexions more favorably. I hated my skin and its color. I had no choice over it. It wasn't until I attended college at the University of Tennessee at Chattanooga that I finally accepted my skin color. I was walking to class the day this revelation took place. I can't say what was unique about this particular walk to class, but it suddenly dawned on me that, "Hey silly, you can't change how dark you are- love yourself." From then on, I never looked down on myself because of my dark skin. It was and is something that will not change. I'm cool with it now, and once I owned it, it worked out for me.

Do you remember the first time you accepted something about yourself that initially caused insecurity? What was that thing, and how did you overcome it? If you're still struggling with it, what do you need to be ok with the person looking back at you in the mirror?

___

___

___

7

DELAYED AWARENESS

First, it was Trayvon Martin, an unarmed Black teen who was gunned down by a white man in Florida. I thought to myself, "Ok, who cares?" Before you drop this book and give up on me, stay the course, and keep reading.

I know that was insensitive of me, but I will make sense of it, I promise. At the time of this killing, I was working at Big Brothers, Big Sisters of Middle Tennessee in Nashville, Tennessee while attending graduate school at Lipscomb University. If anyone knows me, they know that I love Nashville, which is a city whose population is made up primarily of white people, but also a second home to me. Nashville is where I found my independence and developed a better sense of self. I had my first apartment there, started graduate school, found out what it meant to be me, and began to live life just a little bit more fully with the help of Victoria and Chris, two of my best friends.

I remember being in the break room at BBBS, and my co-workers gathered around to hear the verdict of George Zimmerman, the man that murdered Trayvon. I can't say he was found guilty because, unfortunately, he wasn't convicted. But these people gathered to hear something that, in my opinion, they already knew what the outcome would be. I can admit it was heartbreaking to know that this killer was not convicted.

Little did society know; George opened the door for many other killings of unarmed young Black American men within this decade. As history continued to repeat itself, the more it grabbed my attention. I don't know how many young Blacks had to die before I realized this. As a young, Black American man, I have to be aware of myself at all times. I must be knowledgeable of where I am, whom I am with, what I say, how I say it, how I dress, and how others perceive me. I realized that people would judge me merely because of my appearance. What do you think other people judge you for? What are you most afraid of being misperceived about yourself?

___

8

"MR. JUSTIN, YOU BE FRESH."

I once told a group of adolescent males with whom I worked as their therapist, that I just dress how I want to feel that day. I also said to them that you must dress how you want people to perceive you because you already have your skin color against you. As a young, Black American, it is my job to prove you wrong about what you think of me or help you develop a new schema of what it means to be a young Black American.

As we know, being Black and American is complex due to the different thoughts, practices, and beliefs of this culture of people. By no means am I trying to start a movement, but Jessica, Lauren, and Jarrett helped me understand what my color meant to those who did not share the same pigment. I appreciate their friendships, and the energy exchanged there; they gave me many things to think about.

We would often spend our time watching *Scandal* and talking about various issues in the world. They learned quickly that I did not fully understand myself. I had begun to realize I had a different perspective than black people my age. I had gone to predominantly white institutions (PWI) while they all went to historically Black colleges and universities (HBCU). I think the differences came out quickly when we saw the world differently. Their perspectives were refreshing yet enlightening. The moral of the story is recognizing relationships that help you along your journey.

Who keeps you on your toes? Can you name the folks that teach you? What's been the biggest lesson learned?

9

I CAN'T WIN FOR LOSING

These were my words on August 4, 2016, as I listened to Audra Day sing "Rise Up" on the second floor of the Student Union at a university in the southeastern part of the United States. I was processing a conversation I just had with my supervisor on campus. I was pulled aside to learn that several of my Caucasian coworkers in the office were building a case against me with reasons why I should no longer have my job. A position that God had placed me in, not them. I am a firm believer that everything happens for a reason, and God makes no mistakes. If a situation is difficult, the good southern Baptist in me says, it's because something greater is coming, and this is my training for it.

So why did my colleagues think I needed to be terminated? Here is the list my co-workers came up with: (try not to laugh when you read this)
He doesn't speak to me.
He won't add us on Facebook.
Won't he have too much on his plate once the semester starts?
How's he going to handle it all?

Honestly, I would have preferred the complaints to have focused on my actual work ethic instead of several trivial instances. One of my best friends Victoria and I almost found the situation funny, as it reminded us of being in a middle school quarrel. I said I couldn't win for losing, but Victoria quickly stopped my negative thinking, reminding me that I wouldn't fail. I would win. How many of us have them? FRIENDS.

Despite her support, I carried on my morning in the office, angry, anxious, and annoyed. The worst part is that I barely spoke to several co-workers because they choose not to acknowledge or speak to me. If I were walking down the hallway toward a woman in the office, she would look up at the ceiling or walls just to avoid eye contact or having to speak to me. I was so frustrated I wanted to shout, "Ma'am, what the hell are you looking at? Oh, that's right, not my black ass!" Incredibly, the same people who say they feel uncomfortable around me are the same people I have a legitimate reason to fear. It seemed that in our current society, my skin is not light enough to get away with the things they do.

My co-workers watched my every move and chose not to speak to me. Some days I felt invisible, but I was able to come to peace with that. Fortunately for me, while I cannot change my skin color, I can change my thinking and my position. And that is just what I did. My advice to anyone facing hardship, adversity, or an overwhelming situation is you either change your perspective or your position.

Is there anything you need to change your perspective about at this current moment? If so, what is it, and what do you think would change?

___

___

___

___

___

___

___

___

___

___

___

___

10

THE DANGER OF A SINGLE STORY-MY FACE

My co-workers judged me based on how they thought I was, or what they thought I should not be. What those things are, I'm not entirely sure. Honestly, there are so many questions I am unable to answer about the situation, and I am sure if confronted, they wouldn't be able to either. I understand I am contributing to the problem by not generating a conversation about it. Still, then again, it was my workplace. How real can you get before people are finding yet another reason to look at you with scrutiny?

I attended a Multicultural Forum at the University of Memphis that focused on the wrongful deaths of African American men in America. I sat in the room with a mixed group of Caucasians and African Americans. During the forum, a young Caucasian male expressed he was afraid that Blacks would begin treating him differently while thinking he was "one of the bad ones." It was a fascinating perspective. Black people still have more reason to be more afraid of white people than a white person should ever be of anyone that looks like me. I went on to tell him we can challenge that by controlling what's in your immediate reach—treating others with kindness so it can spread like wildfire. If I am honest, I began to give a side-eye at every white male I came in contact with after the many deaths of African American men. Then I realized I didn't want them looking at me in the same manner, so I should stop. This may not solve the problem worldwide, but we have to start somewhere, right? That's my goal to start somewhere. This book isn't to condemn anyone, but to share my experiences in the hope that people of all races are aware of how they fit in society. I find myself fighting a battle that isn't even mine. The fact that my co-workers struggled with me was not my problem to own; it was theirs.

If someone has difficulty working with a disabled person, whose fault is that? The person who can't help their deficiency, or the helper? A disabled individual can't change their physical capabilities. Still, those working with them can change their perspective on how they interact with disabled people. It's the same idea when thinking about race. While skin color isn't an inability, I can't change my race, but others can change their view of how they deal with me.

It is important to remember that being a Black male isn't a deficiency, disorder, or disgrace, far from it. Stereotypes for Black men (or any group of people, for that matter) are incomplete narratives. That one-sided story robs me of how complex I am. We must begin to have the conversations we try to avoid.

In my different classes, I tried to share my experiences of racism, being racially profiled, and how it shaped my views of human behavior. I shared my experience and thoughts in my Advanced Theories class with two white females and one white male. The response I received was empty. I could tell the male was intrigued based on the concerned look on his face and his slight hip tilt. The two women attempted to ask questions but couldn't gather their thoughts. The male stated, "I can relate to that because I don't want to judge my clients based on age." I thought to myself, "What does age have to do with race? Oh wait, I get it. You can understand me being racially profiled because you choose not to judge people based on them being younger than you? Good luck with that."

Again, I'm not sure what I was looking for. Still, when I shared my story, one of the women decided to "let her thoughts sit with her" until she could articulate what she proved to be confusion just moments prior. I walked away from this class exercise understanding that some people aren't able to meet me where I am and show empathy, because they don't know how to with something unfamiliar.

I did not understand why race made others so uncomfortable before this day. Then it dawned on me, race is such a sensitive topic because people are nervous exposing the truth, and at some level, they may feel guilty or are unable to empathize with the struggle of being ostracized. I often tell people; the truth is never a surprise.

Why do you think race causes others to be uncomfortable? Or do you disagree?

11
SEPTEMBER 19, 2016

Terrance Crutcher, an African American man who was also a student, father, and son, was killed outside of his car. He was unarmed, his hands were up, and the police killed him. The next day after learning about this, I cried on my way to work. I cried right in between a hospital and a job site that didn't hire me because I am a Black man. It was symbolic because it no longer mattered that I didn't get the job. I realized that above everything else I was dealing with; my life could be the next one to go.

With each murder of an unarmed Black man, it gets closer and closer to home, no matter the geographical location. I wept while going to work, but I knew I couldn't carry the emotion with me into my office. No one would be there to help me carry the load. No one in the office would ask how I was doing or my thoughts about what's happening.

It seems that my co-workers, who were predominantly Caucasian, cared more about weddings, traffic, or the fact that it rained that day. Although the news continued to show us what was happening in the world, my co-workers didn't acknowledge it.

I understand that personal issues don't matter in the workplace, but my Caucasian female co-worker reported that a dog had attacked her and her dog. The director and his subordinate gathered around her in concern. I thought it couldn't have been that bad if she was recounting the event with a smile. However, some could say that things couldn't have been so bad for me if I were able to make it into work. The difference is, her problems had a space to be discussed and processed at work. My problems did not.

I also found it interesting that everyone believed her when she reported that another dog had attacked her and her dog. When I mentioned this to my boss and others in the office, I was labeled paranoid. If we both see something that made our experience reality, what was the difference? She could be lying about this attack to get attention for all they knew. But it was a safe topic of discussion, and it was important to her.

Can you describe a time where people did not understand and see you? How did that feel, and how did you overcome? How can you overcome it?

_____
_____
_____
_____
_____
_____
_____
_____
_____
_____
_____
_____
_____
_____
_____
_____
_____
_____

12

SOCIAL MEDIA AND A UNIFORM

Social media is a great thing. Sometimes it can be overwhelming, and other times it can be an outlet. As the number of Black men dying from police brutality increased, the more I spoke about it on Facebook. I don't place things on social media to gain likes or shares. However, it is interesting to see that when I speak about God or success, I receive more likes than when I talk about race issues. I will leave it here and ask the question, why do you think this happens?

_____

_____
_____
_____

When the killing of Terrance Crutcher took place, we were offered a chance to speak about it in a class. I was so grateful for that experience. I don't know how else I would have been able to express my thoughts regarding the matter.

A white classmate stated that as a Black man, I wasn't the only person that lives in fear. He went on to say that because he wore a police officer badge, he was fearful people might retaliate against him. That statement could be true, and I agreed that Black men weren't the only ones living in fear. I wanted him to understand that he had a choice to wear the badge or not to wear it; I didn't have that option with my skin color. It's not something I can put on and take off when I want to.

I also knew that if a Black man did retaliate because he was an officer, the Black man would be killed on the spot. However, if my white classmate murdered me, he would get to go home. This isn't about whose problem or fear is bigger. It is about not pretending that history hasn't repeated itself over and over again. He went on to insist that we allow the justice system to work it out. I agree we should, but when the justice system has historically displayed prejudice & unfairness, it's just a repeated cycle.

When has the justice system upset you most? Is there a public case that comes to mind? What about a personal experience? Maybe it is the fear of how the justice system could respond to something that has not happened yet.

13
RAISING A SON

My mother raised me to succeed in life and to be a God-fearing man who treats others with kindness. I wasn't taught how to survive as a Black man in America. Although I'm sure she knew there would be some type of resistance, I never realized that it could lead to my murder once I reached adulthood.

A few years after being racially profiled, I had the chance to speak with my friend who was with me the day the police followed us. I asked him how he experienced this event, and his response was shocking. He stated that he didn't think much about it after that because it did not affect him. I was dumbfounded. I assumed it was as heavy for him as it was for me. He went on to explain that because he grew up poor, Black, and had different exposure than I did, he was used to that type of thing. I also grew up Black and poor, but I had not been exposed to that type of treatment.

It's amazing how two people can share one occurrence but experience it differently. I also grew up poor and Black, but I suppose my experience was different. My understanding is that he was always reminded of his Blackness, while my experience had been the first encounter. His experience with being poor may have been different, but we weren't discussing class, we were discussing race. People have been asked, "When did you realize you were this or that?" We are very seldom asked, "What is your response to how others treat you?"

When did you realize your existence would cause people to treat you differently?

___

___

___

___

___

___

___

___

I was at my internship, speaking with another gentleman who was a white male. I could tell he was trying to make small talk and engage with me. I was just fine with the silence; after all, I am a therapist. However, I responded to his questions in his attempt to get to know me or break the silence. He began asking about the music I listened to while at work. Little did he know I played trap music for two reasons, to tickle my inner hood and to appeal to specific students. Either way, I refused to tell him the truth, so what did I say? "I listen to everything." Everything isn't *everything* when someone begins to name genres of music you have never heard. It was at that moment, I realized how small my musical taste was, or maybe how bad his taste was. The next natural step was to name Drake as an artist I listen to because he is pretty universal, right? I offered that I enjoy 90's R&B. We then started talking about movies.

I recalled a line from *Sister Act*, "Cold beans and collard greens." Everyone knows that, right? WRONG. I realized that when talking about differences in movies and music, I was too ashamed to reveal my real taste out of fear of being misunderstood or embarrassed. Nonetheless, we settled on 90's R&B, which blew out all of the tunes from R. Kelly (who we don't support anymore, just to be clear), Destiny's Child, Usher, and Genuine. I couldn't help but think, "What if a student came in and heard this music? What would they think, and would they blame him or me for these choices?

I volunteered at an event the university hosted where they attempted to vet high school juniors into applying. There I was standing at a table with my female colleague, who was a Caucasian female. Apart from my boss, I was the only male and the only Black male. This was an event where people came around and asked questions about things they would forget by Monday, and the students wouldn't care about by the end of the day. It's one of those things where people come and pick up everything they can as if they are going to read it. I think people often accept something because it's free, not because it has any significance for them.

A young lady was waiting to speak with either my colleague or me. My colleague was busy talking with others, and I was free. I asked the young lady if there was anything I could do for her. She did not acknowledge me or look my way. I did not exist to her. After she spoke with my colleague, we both acknowledged that her waiting to speak was strange. I immediately said, "it's because I'm Black." My co-worker closed her eyes slightly, with her hand on her hip, and gave a chuckle that indicated she was now uncomfortable. She couldn't defend the comment or provide a comforting word. I proceeded to laugh and repeat what I said as if I knew this was the truth. The reality is, I could have reminded her of someone that did something terrible to her, or I could have had morning breath on my lips after 9 am, you name it. But I know as well as any other enlightened individual, it was because I was Black.

14

ANGER

Baldwin once said, "To be a Negro in this country and to be relatively conscious is to be in a rage almost all the time." Anger is what makes our struggle visible. And while I never agreed with the looting that would take place or disasters of protests that would spawn from the killing of unarmed Black men, I grew to understand slightly. Can minorities let go of anger, or is this something that will remain with us due to the injustices of this country? Spiritually speaking (please believe I am no preacher), we are often taught anger does not hurt the other person, it hurts you. What if the thing we are angry about is not directed at a person but a reality? How do we move past this if it is continuously in our peripheral view? I now have the emotional intelligence to know that emotions simply give us information. We have the choice to use that information to make decisions. Do you know what decisions you make when you're happy, sad, mad, or glad?

_____

_____

_____

_____

_____

_____

_____

It was Spring 2017, and I was leading an intensive outpatient group for recovering drug and alcoholic addicts. I would go to the group carrying all the emotions life had allowed me to feel, saddened because I did not like what someone had done to me, or school stressing me out. I took statistics that semester, and anyone that knows me can tell you that I still count on my fingers. I promise that class was made to make me feel dumb or to reveal what form the devil came in. Either way, I found myself sweating and stomach bubbling every time I stepped foot in that class. Now that you know how much I despise math, back to the point.

While leading this group, I was mistaken for another member. I never found myself angry at this because I knew addiction has no face, dress, or disposition- neither does racism. Moral of the story, it is not fair of me or any other minority to treat people who may be racist, negatively. This experience humbled me because after hearing the stories of these clients, maybe my "issues" were not as significant as I perceived. Don't get me wrong; statistics gave me the blues, and my friends were not always nice, but sometimes it takes another human being to show you that we all hurt. We all see pain during this life, no matter the face attached to it.

One day before work while ironing my clothes (which I should do at night with how I rush in the morning), this hit me: I cannot get rid of being Black! So when people connect various situations to race, it is because we cannot rid ourselves of what is the truth.

What do I mean by this? Sometimes people wonder why I attribute adverse events to being Black. It is because it could very well be a correct assumption. Think about it. If something you carry with you is disliked and judged, how can you avoid considering this is the reason you were treated a particular way?

For instance, I watched a video that went viral on Facebook in October 2017, where a white man yelled at the police (a fellow white man), ran from him, and then ran towards the officer after being tased. He then proceeded to steal the police officer's car. Someone in internet land put together side by side videos of that encounter, next to a Black man who appeared to be calm while being arrested by the police. During this arrest, he decided to run and was shot in the back. This man was much older than the white man in the other video. While multiple police officers were arresting the older Black man, the white man was only being captured by one. It would have made more sense for the officer who was alone to use force to apprehend his criminal than for the Black man to be shot when someone could have simply run after him. Now, was running from the police smart? Absolutely not, but the force used was not equal, especially when comparing videos.

Let's look at this from a different viewpoint. I recently applied for a position on campus that I was very qualified for. Out of 200 applicants, I made it to the top three candidates and did not get the job over a white woman. Now, could she have been more qualified than me and had a better interview, yes. But then as a Black man sitting across from two privileged white men with power, I can't help but think, did I not get this job due to the way I look?

Now don't think I am comparing not getting a job over someone getting shot. What I am saying is that was the Black man shot because he was Black while the white man suffered no harm? Did I not get the job because I am Black, or was I less qualified? These are questions that we know the answer to but can never prove. How you feel in the moment can hardly be explained and not widely understood. The frustration of people thinking you are crazy or irrational for asking that type of question is even more annoying. Because I cannot rid myself of my melanin, which I love, by the way, I would instead embrace it.

We are tasked with avoiding the use of race as an excuse, while not continually perpetuating the angry Black person stereotype. Unfortunately, we are labeled as "angry Black people" when we hold our tongues in the face of ignorance. Just like the Vegas shooting that took place in 2017, racism is like bullets coming at us, and we don't know which direction it will come from next. It feels like our backs are against the wall sometimes. It isn't miserable to live this life, just a little more challenging.

If you want a Black man to feel small or angry, put him in contact with a white man who uses his privilege to his advantage. My very first boss, while working for the university, was just that; old, white, privileged. He was more aware of that privilege and less aware of how he made me feel. He was by far the worst boss I ever had. One of the lessons I took away was to be a leader once I have a position like his, to not just be in charge of others. I have never hated anyone in life until I came face to face with him. I am sure that he was there to teach me a lesson on how to navigate through corporate America or job politics, but I was never good with difficult lessons when it came to race.

Some days, much like the day I wrote this, he left me feeling angry at how he spoke to me, made me feel dismissed, had an accusatory tone as if I should know what he was talking about when his directions were unclear. I started to pray for my attitude to change, so I would not continue to carry so much hate around with me. As a Christian growing up with my mother, I was taught that hate was bad. This was a value I wanted to hold on to as an adult. I started to search for how I could handle working with him. When I saw him, I would go the other way, sit in my car a little longer to avoid having to talk to him, or even walk faster to avoid awkward, forced conversations.

The most interesting part was, I believe he was aware of his problem with Blacks, although he would never admit it. He carried on because he knew no matter his bias, he still had power. Little did he know, I was on the search for how I could find my power. I was aware I made him nervous, as evidenced by him working up the nerve to address me in the beginning phases of my job. He would pace outside of my office before talking to me and had the type of heavy breathing when giving a speech in front of people. I would not call what I had power; I would just call it being Black while he was uncomfortable—nothing profound there, just an observation.

15

CONVERSATIONS WITH A YOUNG BLACK MAN

One day I agreed to stay after work to advise one of my freshmen students who happened to be Black. Among the many things we discussed that day, like majors and classes, we also talked about accountability for his behavior, discipline, and identity. We talked about his perception of racism in America. This young man believed that all white people were racist. I listened to him and tried to understand his perspective. When it was my turn to speak, I acknowledged his belief and explained why I disagreed. At the time, one of my co-workers was pregnant and expecting a baby girl in the upcoming weeks. I said to him; there is no way that baby will be born racist. In my eyes, all babies and children are perfect. Racism, to me, doesn't develop until people do one of two things:

1. Fail to identify, acknowledge, and understand their privilege, which causes a blind eye to important causes.
2. Use their privilege to their advantage to make others feel small and incapable.

I wanted him to understand that there are some outstanding people out there, and there are some terrible people as well. However, the Black race can't afford to treat every person that doesn't look like them as if they were the first person to have wronged them. Living life as a minority is always balancing anger or frustration, withholding the tongue while consistently exhibiting humility and gratitude. Why humility and gratitude? Think about it. Where would you be if it weren't for those who came before you? Where would you be without your higher power and your parents (whether they were good or bad)? They either influenced you to be like them or encouraged you to be better.

I wanted to encourage him on that day to allow himself to be 19 years of age and let it play out; however it may. To be at peace with whoever showed up when he looked in the mirror. I often told students that college is not about the difficulty; it is about finding out who you are and how you fit in the world, embracing challenges as they come your way- you happen to get a degree in the meantime.

Let us all take a moment and smile, knowing that we are all great in our own right no matter how we were born. Whether you are lactose intolerant, have a fifth toe, or you sweat a lot, and it shows through your shirt when you're trying to flirt. Laugh a little? Great! If not, read that sentence over again. What advice would you give your younger self?

_____
_____
_____
_____
_____
_____
_____
_____
_____
_____
_____
_____
_____
_____

16

WHAT DO I DO WITH THIS MESS?

What do you do when you fall and get dirty? You get up, dust off, and keep going. Just like when I hold my tongue to keep my job, I change my perspective to stay alive. To avoid getting arrested or to be another angry person looking for a fight, to only still feel empty.

I don't want to be one who complains over and over about issues. So let's discuss how does one see the mess, sit in the mess, and get past it? It's easy to clean up a child who has fallen; you dust their little butts off and keep moving. How do you dust off a bruised ego, a broken heart, or frustration? I may not be able to come up with a cure for you, but for me, it is a change in perspective. It is understanding the Knobbman theory, what do I bring into this room?

Let's break it down:
Male
Black Bald
Decent-looking Slim
Clean cut Intelligent
Slightly urban
Awkward

Notice I started with things that people can see. Why is that? Unfortunately, that is how we kick off interactions with others. We judge people based on outside appearances before we allow ourselves to listen, observe, and develop judgment from what is instead of what appears to be.

Once we sit down and accept what we have, what we carry, then we can start to realize how people see us. I can't help that I am a male and Black and would not want to, so what do I do? Embrace that. There is no need to be angry with others or a system if you are too busy being unhappy with what is yours, your identity.

Now identify what you bring into a room before you even say anything. What does this mean to you, and how do you think others perceive it?

After we conceptualize how others see us, we will gain clarity. I remember my first semester in graduate school at Lipscomb University. Keep in mind; I was the only Black male in the class. The instructor talked about race and how, when working with clients, you will not see race. I remember feeling anxious in response to his statement because my friend Heather who sat next to me, was white. I spoke up and said, "I don't agree with that." I see that Heather is white just as much as she sees that I am Black. Of course, you see race, it's apparent. If you don't (which isn't possible), others do, as evidenced by the looks we get when we are out in public together. It does not bother us, but we see our physical differences. The key is we choose to keep walking and not allow our differences to interfere with our friendship. That is how we can all get along.

Do you consider yourself to see color in others? How does race impact your engagement with people?

_____
_____
_____
_____
_____
_____
_____
_____
_____

17

I LITERALLY HATED HIM: VALUES AND HATE

On this particular day, I worked out with my best friend, Chris. While telling him about my frustrations with my now former boss, he could also identify with my experience. He has also struggled with racism or "pissing matches" working for men. He agreed that I needed to let this hate go that I desperately wanted to release, but neither of us had a solution. I just appreciated that someone could relate.

I went to bed that night and woke up in prayer. I asked God to allow me to show kindness, rid me of this anger, and prevent it from interfering with my job or destiny. Some people said I should kill it with kindness, but the word I spoke during my morning Prayer was GRACE. Yes, grace is what I needed to show others as I would want it shown to me. So I need to put on my big boy shoes and be nice, not through gritted teeth, but with ease and calm.

I got to work after this great prayer and still did not quite hit the head on the target. I walked right past him and failed to speak. The grimace on my face was guilt and thoughts of failure. I just had to commit and accept this attitude change. There needed to be a shift in my thinking so my behavior could follow- a little cognitive triangle there for my fellow counselors. At that moment, I realized, we expect adolescents to change their behavior after a session or two, but as an adult, I could barely get my act together. What was going on?

This issue was more prominent and more profound than merely saying I was going to make a quick attitude adjustment. So I sat and pondered at my desk. Should I confront my boss and tell him I believe he is a racist? No, of course not. However, for something to bother me to this magnitude meant this was serious. I think I was starting to feel the emotions and aggression from years of not realizing what it meant to be someone who looked like me.

Here I was at a job paying for my degree, a simple job, one that allowed me to work with students and build relationships. This job allowed me to mentor students from all walks of life. It provided the opportunity to gain experience in higher education, which I always thought I wanted. And yet somehow, I was miserable all because of this white, privileged man.

The story I told myself was it his goal was to break me, to see me fail, and I was allowing him to win. Why was that? Was I unconsciously feeding into what was expected of me? Or was this the reality of working for someone like him? So many questions at this moment, but no answers. Having no answers was hard for someone like me, who seeks clarity in everything I do. I was seeking a solution that wasn't in a textbook. An answer that could not come from my co-workers or even a parent. I needed to get to the bottom of this myself.

I decided that instead of marching into his office and giving a speech, I would write about it. If I were to speak to him, it would go something like this:

"Hey, do you have a minute? I have been struggling with something lately and believe that being honest and transparent with you may help me heal from this. I hate you, and I don't want to hate you. I know you did not want to hire me because of my race (someone on the hiring committee told me that), but God saw fit for me to be here. I stand affirmed in knowing what is for me is for me, and no one can block that. In my first seven months, you used my supervisor, who you paired me with because we were both Black, to speak to me about your thoughts. You didn't like the way I did things, and even though my work wasn't incorrect, you saw an issue with it. I remember when you would pace up and down the hallway in front of my office before building the nerve to speak to me about some- thing. I could hear the anxiety in the shortness of your breath.

Then in my evaluation, I stated that no one would know how it felt to be a Black man in this office, and you blamed me for how others treated me instead of taking ownership of the problem. This was the culture you created within the office. I know it is wrong to hate people, which is partially why I want to stop this. The other reason being is that it doesn't help me, and it will not prevent you from being who you are. I just want to be given a fair shot at being great here.

I have noticed that while you are in charge, you are not a leader. If anything, you have taught me how not to be in my career. I also want to apologize because I have given you too much credit for having power over my life. God has power, you do not, and that has nothing to do with you and everything to do with me. I will choose to lean into my faith and know what is meant to be for me, will be, and there is nothing you can do to stop it.

I will continue to show up on time for work, do the job, follow the rules, be professional, and set an example for our student workers. But today, I choose to stop allowing you to have so much control in my head and know that this is not the prize. You and others here have decided to make this job your life because you have nothing else, but my destiny is much bigger than this.

I appreciate the lessons because I am sure they will come in handy one day, but I need to be done with this. A very wise friend told me to simply keep my eye on the prize. That is what I intend to do. Thanks for listening. I don't expect you to say anything back because I am afraid that anything that escapes your mouth right now would be a lie. An attempt to save face all through a shaky voice and poor eye contact.

I will get back to work now, oh, and trust that I can do more than what you think I can. Just like the time you didn't believe I wrote something myself simply because you were impressed. My job isn't to impress you; my job is to positively influence students and guide them correctly so they can use these tools when they need them the most. "

Through my writing, I have found therapy. Through my writing, I have found a way to say what I want without risking my job, self-respect, or anything else.

Think of an event, person, or experience that you want to address. What would you say if you had the chance to change the hate in your heart?

18
CONTINUING THE CONVERSATION: SOLUTIONS

It was November 2017 that I presented on this topic at an Empowering Men's Conference, which highlighted areas of culture, identity, academics, education, business, and finance. The description of my class goes as follows:

Navigating your Black: Students will share various experiences of being a man of color in college. Students will talk about the challenges faced, including negative perceptions, responding to adversity, and address stigmas associated with their image in college. Students will complete two activities to examine commonalities and differences among each other.

Luckily it went well, and I received great feedback. One of the participants in the class was a 52-year-old man with his teenage son, who had recently begun driving. The father expressed concern that we were having a conversation regarding issues that he faced when he was a child. Someone else in the class asked me, "How do we challenge others and respond to adversity?" I responded by saying we first have to treat adversity like a relationship and pick our battles. If I respond to racism or negativity daily, I would be exhausted.

1. We first have to be aware of who we are and embrace our skin color.
2. We have to acknowledge what it means to carry our skin color.
3. We have to pick our battles but have the courage to educate others when necessary.

4. We have to start with treating everyone with kindness because everyone isn't George Zimmerman or Dylann Roof.
5. Finally, we have to know and be at peace with knowing that all people will not understand, so be aware of your audience and know when to walk away.

Each day we get up and go after something. If we continue to put one foot in front of the other, we will eventually get to where we want to go. I graduated as the first Black male to obtain a Masters in Professional Counseling from Lipscomb University. I was the first Black male to earn a Doctorate in Philosophy from the University of Memphis in Counselor Education and Supervision. All of this occurred after seeing my father pass away the day before my tenth birthday, struggling with self-esteem, being the recipient of bullying, struggling with identity, being told by my high school guidance counselor that I was not smart enough to attend college, not having a Black man to mentor on my educational journeys, and being raised by a single parent. I accomplished my goals by learning to love myself, not seeking external affirmation, being confident in my decisions, finding my voice, and finally accepting who existed in my skin. I continued to put one foot in front of the other, day after day. I had the courage of a single freckle. Change starts with the courage of one person and guided by an army of many. What do you need to be courageous about, and who is your army?

_____
_____
_____
_____
_____
_____
_____

Connect with Justin K. Dodson on the following platforms:

Facebook: Justin Keith

Instagram: @itsdrjkeith

www.ingramcontent.com/pod-product-compliance
Lightning Source LLC
Chambersburg PA
CBHW071223070526
44584CB00019B/3139